YOUR $1500 FRUGAL WEDDING

A Simple Guide to Getting What You Want - From Touching Ceremony to Fun Getaway

RACHEL HATHAWAY

Also available in audiobook format, narrated by Jackie Lauper
www.yourfrugalwedding.com

ISBN-13: 978-1547218868
ISBN-10: 154721886X

✱ Created with Vellum

Contents

Frugal Wedding

Preface

Uncover the secrets to having the wedding you deserve for $1,500 or less.

The average wedding costs about $30,000. But it doesn't have to.

Learn creative money-saving ideas, resources, and tips to keep your beautiful, romantic, and memorable wedding from costing you a fortune.

Instead of spending thousands on one day, have the wedding of your dreams and still have the resources to:

- have a fun honeymoon getaway
- buy a house

- get out of debt
- start your married life together on secure financial footing

You want your wedding to be memorable and fun for you, your fiancee, and your guests, and you want to do it without breaking the bank.

So let's get started...

Frugal Wedding

Introduction

You're engaged?!?! [*high-pitched girlie squeal*] I am so happy for you!!! Seriously! Just thinking about you, happy reader, and the fact that you have found the love of your life, and the fact that the love of your life was smart enough to realize that you are the love of your sweetheart's life, makes me smile.

Congratulations!

Now that you two lovebirds have told your family, friends, and acquaintances, and your mother has told her family, friends, and acquaintances, and you've started using your left hand far more often just to gaze at / show off your newly acquired accessory, you've slowly and gently fluttered down from cloud nine to realize that now you actually have to...

...PLAN A WEDDING!

For most people, implementing a wedding will be the most complicated thing you ever do; not just because there are so many moving parts, but because there is an overwhelming pressure and desire to make your wedding personal and memorable. Legendary, even.

Weddings have evolved from routine events where people knew exactly what to expect, to completely customized extensions of the couple's personalities. For some, "traditional" weddings have even become unpopular, frowned upon as uncreative and bland.

Because of this, planning a wedding will probably be the first true test for the newly engaged couple. It can get very stressful balancing your tastes, your sweetie's tastes, logistical limitations, as well as the expectations of family, friends, and society, all the while trying to put your creative stamp on every aspect of the wedding.

And that's not even mentioning the budget. If you're one of those organized types who's had a binder since sixth grade of your ideal wedding, you may be in for a bit of shell shock when you start tallying up the cost of that dream wedding.

Here's the thing.

YES, your wedding IS one of the most important days of your life.

BUT... it's important because this is the day that your lives offlcially become connected. This is the day that you announce, publicly, in front of people who love you, that you are committed to each other through the good and the bad. This is the day that you are no longer just dating; this is the day that you are MARRIED.

And frankly, that's all anyone attending your wedding really cares about. They just want to see you and your sweetie happy. As long as you're smart about your guest list, no one at your wedding will be judging your centerpiece or menu choices. These are people who love you, and would be equally happy seeing you married in your backyard in your pajamas as on a private island resort or picturesque vineyard.

Is the dress important?

No. It's important that YOU FEEL BEAUTIFUL.

Is the venue important?

No. It's important that EVERYONE YOU LOVE IS THERE.

Are the favors important?

No. It's important that EVERYONE FEELS VALUED.

Catch my drift?

As long as you both keep things within this perspective, planning and executing a wedding can be lots of fun, and the sense of accomplishment when you see people having fun at your wedding is enough to make your heart burst.

Alright. Enough of that warm and fuzzy talk. Let's start saving.

How to Use This Book

Each chapter in this book is set up with the following sections:

- **Frugal Wedding Budget Option** - This is the suggestion for the most economical way of handling that aspect of the wedding, and the best way to stay within your $1,500 budget.
- **Keep Your Cash Tips** - This is a list of ideas and suggestions if you decide on a different option than the Frugal Wedding Budget option.

Each chapter also makes the following assumptions:

- **You have to hire someone** - While I mention in multiple places throughout this book the importance of leveraging the skills, labor, and relationships of your friends and family, the Frugal Wedding Budget options given in each chapter assume you don't know anyone who can fill that role for you. After all, if your network consists of a professional cake decorator, graphic designer, wedding planner, photographer, florist, seamstress, hair stylist, restaurant owner, chef, musician, and pastor, then you shouldn't have any worries about paying for your wedding! Hopefully you'll have at least one of these covered by someone in your circle of friends and family, but these suggestions are for those of you who aren't lucky enough to be surrounded by wedding professionals.
- **You're paying** - Along those same lines, I'm assuming you and your sweetheart are paying for everything. Even though traditionally the couple's parents would provide a significant amount of financial assistance, more couples are paying for their weddings out of pocket these days. If

someone in your lives offers to help pay for your Big Day, by all means, give them a hearty yes and an equally hearty hug! But remember that if someone else is paying, you can't get too picky about what they're buying. And while you shouldn't count on cash gifts as part of your wedding budget, don't forget that you are almost guaranteed to get some money from your guests, which can go a long way toward refllling that bank account.

Where'd You Get Those Numbers?

The average costs provided in this book are based on national averages pulled from various reliable sources. The actual cost may be less or more in your area. This goes for the estimated budgeted costs for each Frugal Wedding Budget option as well. The numbers provided for each Frugal Wedding Budget option aren't intended to be strict, one-size-flts-all; they're just guidelines. Depending on your priorities and tastes, your budget may look different than that offered in this book, which is as it should be.

Speaking of budget...

Frugal Wedding

Your Budget

IF YOU'VE DONE ANY RESEARCH INTO WEDDING costs, you've probably run across the statistic that the average American wedding costs between $25,000-$30,000, not including the honeymoon.

THIRTY THOUSAND DOLLARS! Yikes.

Imagine someone hands you a check for $30,000. Are you REALLY going spend it on a party that lasts - on average - five hours?

If you're reading this book, you've likely already made the decision not to spend that much cash. But just in case you're still on the fence, consider this: The wedding website TheKnot in conjunction with the e-commerce site PayPal conducted a survey and found that more than one-third of couples go into debt to pay for their wedding, using credit cards or loans. Do you really want to be paying for that $1,200 wedding dress six months from now when it's just taking up space in your closet?

And even if you have the money to cash flow this expense, is spending it on a gala event the best use of that cash? Or would it be better spent as a downpayment for a house? Or a rainy day fund? Or pay down your debt?

If I still haven't convinced you, a study by two economics professors at Emory University found that couples who spend less on their wedding tend to have longer lasting marriages than those who spend more.

So there. Any way you slice it, saving money is the smarter thing to do, and there are TONS of ways to save on your wedding.

According to several sources, here's a breakdown of the national average costs for the various aspects of a wedding in the U.S.:

Wedding Planner: $1,800
Rehearsal Dinner: $1,100
Ceremony/Reception Venue: $15,100
Limousine: $730

Catering: $8,580 ($66/person x avg. guest count
of 130)
Cake: $540
Invitations: $440
Dress: $1,200
Tuxedo: $250
Rings (Engagement/Wedding): $7,100
Florist/Decor: $2,000
Favors: $280
Officiant: $260
Photographer: $2,400
Videographer: $1,700
Reception Music/Band: $3,400
Ceremony Music: $600
Reception DJ: $1,000

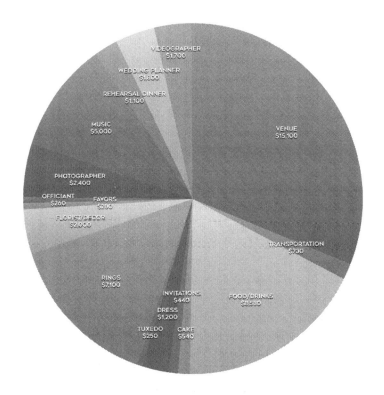

National Average Wedding Costs in the USA

If you were to follow this trend, your wedding would cost $48,480!!

We can do better than that!

Here are a few guiding principles that will help keep your budget low:

1. Decide what your priorities are.

When planning a wedding on a budget, you're going to have to be flexible, but if you know there are one or two non-negotiables, account for them, and figure out how you can compensate in other areas. Do you have a huge family and know that your guest list is 200 people easy? Then maybe opt for a potluck dinner instead of catering. Is it not really a wedding in your mind if it's not in a church? Unless your church will do it for free or a discounted rate, you may need to forego the formal fforal arrangements.

The traditional rule of thumb is that the costs of your food (including drinks, but not cake) and venue combined should account for no more than half of your total budget, but depending on your ultimate budget and circumstance, this may not apply to you.

2. Decide what kind of wedding you want.

Do you and your sweetie prefer a formal feel, or are you laid back? Do you love a rustic aesthetic, or vintage? Deciding on an overall character and tone for your wedding will help prevent you from feeling overwhelmed, as well as steer you toward money-saving ideas.

3. Keep it Simple

For some reason, there are people who think that a wedding isn't complete without all of the expensive trappings: arches, pew ribbons, confetti, twinkle lights, boutineers, bouquets... the list goes on and on.

Obviously this is not realistic if you're planning a wedding on a budget. Take a good, hard look at everything included in a "typical" wedding, and decide whether it's truly going to add anything to your Big Day. The less stuff needed for your happy event, the less you will have to buy - and the less stuff you'll have left over to deal with after the fact.

4. Take advantage of your network.

Don't be afraid to ask for help. Believe it or not, the people around you want to help. If you know someone who is a graphic designer, ask them (nicely!) if they can design your invitations. If your sister works at a craft store, ask her to go shopping with you to get her employee discount. Does your mom have a membership at the local wholesale retailer like BJ's or Costco? Go shopping with her and see what kinds of deals you can find. Chances are you know at least one person - or someone in your network knows someone - who has a skill or situation that will help you save money. Not to mention free labor setting up/taking down chairs and tables, creating a centerpiece assembly line, and saving on delivery charges by sending your friends or family to pick up the cake, ffowers, etc.

Obviously, don't take advantage of people. And it's just good manners to budget for a little extra gift for those who are doing you a favor, especially those who are giving you a service for free that they usually charge for, like musicians or photographers; spending $100 on gift cards for friends and family who helped you is a lot cheaper than paying their professional rates.

5. Stay organized.

Having an economical wedding means you will be doing a lot of the work yourself. I cannot stress enough how important keeping yourself (and your helpful team of friends and family!) organized is. The worst nightmare of any bride is to wake up the day of the wedding and realize you forgot some critical detail.

Research, planning, and execution of the myriad aspects of your wedding can get overwhelming if you don't keep track of everything. Plus, if you don't monitor your spending, you could go over budget! Eek!

Do it however you want - a simple notebook, a binder, a spreadsheet, a website, an app - whatever tool you can use to keep yourself organized. Personally, I prefer

Google Drive or Evernote, but use what works best for you.

However you end up tracking, make sure you have dedicated sections for each aspect of the wedding, and make sure you write everything down, including which decisions you have to make first (venue!), who is responsible for what, budgeted cost, actual expenditures, different options, cost comparisons, delivery dates, etc.

6. Keep your guest count low.

This saves money in so many ways! You'll spend less on food, you won't need as many chairs and tables, and you can manage a smaller venue. A good rule of thumb is to only invite friends who know - or have at least met - both of you. Also consider having an adults-only wedding, which will reduce not only the guest count but the likelihood of temper tantrums ruining your romantic ceremony or magical first dance.

If you're having a hard time paring it down, consider only inviting your closest friends and immediate family, which prevents distant relatives and acquaintances from feeling slighted when they find out they weren't invited. There's also a growing trend of having the actual wedding ceremony private or family-only, and then throwing a big, casual celebration with a repetition of the vows (or not) the following summer for those who missed it the first time round.

7. Embrace used stuff.

There is an average of 2.3 million weddings per year. And you can bet a whole lot of those couples end up going home with extra centerpieces, decorations, and favors. Not to mention all of those dresses hanging in closets. Set alerts on CraigsList, eBay, Tradesy, and other reputable websites for good deals on wedding stuff. Just make sure to compare prices of used items to their actual retail cost - some people think you're going to help them recoup 100% of their investment.

Also, if the item is going to be shipped to you, try asking for pictures of the items from multiple angles to make sure it will work for you and that there are no defects. Established websites like eBay have pretty solid return policies, but you don't want to waste time on sending stuff back and starting your search all over again.

Some people feel creeped out by the thought of buying used items, especially clothing. Don't be. There are *so many* reasons buying anything used is better than buying new:

- WAY CHEAPER! - Pretty much anything used is going to be less expensive than new.
- Better Quality - Used clothing is less likely to shrink in the wash because it's already been washed. And you can rest assured that if something is used and it still looks good, it's of a high quality and will continue to look good for you, rather than taking a gamble on brand new clothes that will start falling apart after you wear them twice.
- Supporting Your Local Community - Money spent at smaller second-hand stores is more likely to remain in your community than if you spend it at a national chain. Some thrift stores, like Savers or Salvation Army, even have relationships with local charities, so shopping there is supporting a good cause.
- Better for the Environment - Buying used supports the used goods industry, which reduces the amount of landflll waste. Decreasing demand for new items means less consumption of resources and reduced global shipping emissions. Bonus!
- Did I mention that used stuffiis WAY CHEAPER!!

If you're still not convinced, remember that people

often donate brand new clothing and items with the tag still on it to second-hand stores. These items will still be severely marked down from the retail cost, so you can support the cycle of reuse and save money without having any case of the creeps.

8. Think local and in-season.

Do a little research to find out which foods and flowers are ripe and blooming naturally in your area at the time of your wedding. If you're getting married in winter, then a strawberry-filled cake and a bouquet of daisies aren't the most budget-conscious choices.

Along those lines, because of increased demand, flowers cost more (as in 15% to 30% more) near Easter, Mother's Day, Valentine's Day, and prom season, so try to keep your wedding far, far away from these holidays.

9. Shop the sales, and don't the forget coupons!

Take a close look at those junk mail flyers before you recycle them, as they often include notices of sales in your neighborhood. Every time there's a holiday, there is a clearance sale immediately after:

- Valentine's Day - great for decorations such as vases and ribbon
- Easter - look for baskets, pretty stationery, flower girl dresses, and shoes for everyone in the wedding party
- Fourth of July - perfect stufffor your outdoor wedding: tiki torches, flatware, and outdoor tablecloths
- Halloween - black vases, pumpkins
- Thanksgiving - beautiful decorations for your fall wedding
- Christmas - think lights, greenery, and tablecloths

Before you go to any store, be sure to check their website for coupons. Craft stores, big box stores, you name it - they almost all have coupons on their website, or will send you one if you sign up for their newsletter.

Many stores now have their own coupon apps, with coupons that may not be available on their website. If a coupon is only good for a limited number of items per visit, bring a friend (or two, or five!) and make separate purchases to get the most out of your shopping trips so you don't have to waste gas going to the store over and over.

10. Save big with rebate and discount websites.

Websites such as FatWallet (see our resource chapter at the end) give you rebates on purchases made through their site. Amazon also has Amazon Warehouse, which sells open-box items or items with damaged packaging at discounted rates. Get discounted gift cards at Raise for the stores you're going to shop at, and set alerts so you'll know as soon as a new card is available.

11. Venture outside of your usual shopping places.

Drive around your neighborhood and look at all of the stores you don't usually go to. Stop in and see what they have to offer - especially if you see the word "SALE" in their window!

If you're like me, you frequent the big box stores where you can get everything in one trip. While you may not usually shop at dollar stores or discount stores, these places may have what you're looking for at lower prices. Don't drive around too much though - you don't want to spend all your savings on gas.

Look online as well at your regular retail stores and those other stores; you may find even better selection, but don't let shipping costs eat into your savings.

12. Use your credit card points.

If you have a credit card with cash back points and 0% APR, then go ahead and charge as much as you can. Just DON'T FORGET to pay it back BEFORE the interest charges kick in though.

13. Give yourself plenty of time.

There's no getting around it: Planning a wedding on a budget just takes longer than spending haphazardly. You want to be able to take advantage of seasonal and clearance sales at stores, compare prices, as well as leave yourself (and Team Wedding) time to make any DIY wedding projects. Spreading out the expenses over a year also feels a lot less painful than spending it all in three months.

14. Saving money doesn't have to mean skimping on style.

Just because your wedding isn't going to cost a gazillion dollars doesn't mean it can't look like it did. This goes hand in hand with the "give yourself time" concept, because getting things to look beautiful and stylish will take a lot of creativity and experimentation.

15. Be realistic.

You can't do everything. Being realistic about your time, abilities, and preferences will help keep planning and executing your wedding an enjoyable experience. If you don't like doing crafts, then don't try to make your own invitations. If you've never really baked before, don't try to make your cake.

If you do want to do everything, and you do actually have the appropriate skill sets, be realistic about your timeline. Floral arrangements, making the cake, and decorating the venue are just a few of the activities that need to happen the day before or day of the wedding. You can't wear yourself ragged and be too exhausted to enjoy your own wedding. Don't be afraid to delegate to friends or family, or spend a little money early in the process to reduce last minute stress.

16. Think about after the wedding.

Even if you don't spend much, it's a bummer to buy something you're only going to use once. Buying items you know you can use again will give you that much more bang for your buck.

If you can't use something again, sell it! Continue the cycle of Happy Couples helping Happy Couples.

17. Remember, this is YOUR wedding.

While it's wonderful that people want to help, sometimes they feel that they need to offer their opinions as well. You don't have to hold the ceremony at a certain venue simply because your parents were married there, and you don't have to buy the dress that your sister insists is perfect for you even though it's way too expensive. You and your lovey are the only ones who truly matter here. Thank others for their advice and move on.

Now that we've covered the big picture stuff, let's talk details...

2

Frugal Wedding

Venue & Transportation

Wedding Venue

National Average Cost: $15,100

THE VENUE IS THE FIRST WEDDING DECISION YOU need to make. If you've started looking around for places to have your wedding, you know that there are lots of options. Many cities and towns offer a variety of event centers, halls, and churches, but they'll charge you for tablecloths and chair upgrades, add on cleaning fees, and request even more money if you want to serve alcohol. A lot of venues will even require you to use their approved vendors, such as DJs, caterers, and bartenders, immediately upping the cost.

So what do you do...?

Outdoor Wedding
Your Frugal Wedding Budget: $0 - $300

Outdoor venues, such as a local park or farm, require little or no decoration and usually don't cost a thing. A gazebo in someone's well-landscaped backyard, or even a garden nursery center (which is also usually tented - bonus!), can be a perfect setting for your wedding.

Consider scouting ceremony sites at a local lake or beach if you live near one; it's simple and classic. Just make sure it's very clear in the invitations that the wedding in on a beach, so people come prepared with appropriate footwear (or lack thereof).

State and national parks can provide a beautiful background, and many of them have pavilions you can use for your reception. Some also have playgrounds, so any children of your guests will have instant entertainment. Ask about parking fees and recreation permit fees, which can run pretty high. There is a caveat here: Be sure to check out the restroom facilities - not all park bathrooms are created equal.

Of course, an outdoor wedding is always subject to mother nature, and you'll need to factor in the cost of reserving - and potentially using - a large tent, which can take a big chunk out of your budget.

Check out other local attractions that could provide a unique venue for your wedding, such as a zoo, botanical garden, historical site, or museum. Some of these may charge a small fee or donation, and others may not. You'll have to call and check around, because each one will be different.

If you belong to a church, you may be able to use the building for free, or pay a small fee to use an adjacent hall or room for your reception.

Whichever venue you decide on, make sure you book it early. You must have the date confirmed before you make any other plans. Some venues may book up fast depending on the time of year (September and October are currently the most popular months for marriages), and you may not get the date you desire if you don't act quickly.

Keep Your Cash Tips

If the frugal outdoor wedding isn't for you, here are some other ways you can save money on your venue:

All-in-One - Having your ceremony and your reception at the same venue not only saves money but time and stress as well. Simply ask your ushers to move back a few of the tables to make a dance floor. Your guests won't have to travel to a reception (this is especially good for out-of-town or elderly guests), and you won't have to pay twice.

Choose your date wisely - Saturday is the most expensive day to have a wedding. Ask your desired venue about their Sunday or weekday rates. Yes, weekday weddings are unexpected, but everyone will have plenty of notice to take the day off. Unless they're willing to help pay for the venue fee, don't let anyone's mutterings of discontent bother you! A weekday wedding can also be less expensive for people who have to travel, as rates are generally lower during the week.

Getting married in the off-season will also save you on venue costs. June through September are peak wedding months and therefore the most expensive, with winter months being the cheapest. Just like weddings have an off-season, wedding professionals do too, so you'll save on photographers, musicians, and others.

Rent a house - Finding a beautiful house for the weekend in a lovely area is super easy on sites like AirBNB. Not only will it serve as the perfect wedding venue, it can be reception hall and honeymoon suite as well. Being upfront that you'll be using their house in this way, and maintaining good communication with the homeowner will ensure a positive experience on both sides.

Colleges and Universities - If you live near a historic college campus, chances are the dining hall is gorgeous with wood beams, high ceilings, and a gigantic fireplace. Or maybe they have a chapel on campus you can reserve on the cheap. If you know an employee, alumni, or current student, have them make the call to see if they'll get a discount.

Tables & Chairs

National Average Cost: $354-1,670

Even if you've found the right venue, your guests need a place to sit, eat, and visit with each other. You can contact a rental company for this, but their prices might be a little more than you're willing to pay. They may also charge you a fee if the tables and chairs aren't immaculate when you return them.

Borrow/Rent from Church or Lodge
Your Frugal Wedding Budget: $50

Local lodges, like the Elks, VFW, or American Legion, always have a lot of tables on hand. Contact the ones in your area to see if they would be willing to rent them to you and how much they would charge. You will probably need to have a way to pick them up and return them, so make sure you have a friend with a truck if you can't do it yourself. Churches are also prepared for large gatherings, and may be willing help you out either for free or a small fee. Again, you'll probably need to transport them yourself.

Keep Your Cash Tips

The Bigger the Better - The bigger your tables are, the fewer centerpieces and tablecloths you'll need.

Tablecloths - If your tables are free or inexpensive, you may need to spend some money on tablecloths, as they may not match or be in perfect condition. Tablecloths will hide these inconsistencies and stains, and your guests will never know the difference.

Check out post-holiday clearance sales for table coverings, and be sure to look at party stores and dollar stores as well. If you're having difficulty finding tablecloths that aren't too expensive, you could always make your own. Go to craft stores and find fabric on sale that matches your wedding colors. Some stores even have clearance fabrics for as low as a dollar per yard, which makes a pretty cheap tablecloth. Just hem up the edges (or have a friend do it).

Rule of Thumb - When you're counting up the chairs and tables you'll need, overestimate by 10%. This will accommodate any guests that didn't RSVP but decided to show up anyway. It also leaves enough space for anyone you have hired (such as a photographer, DJ, or officiant) to sit down and eat.

Transportation

National Average Cost: $730

Drive Yourself
Your Frugal Wedding Budget: $0

Do you really need a stretch limo SUV or horse-drawn carriage? Think about your entrance and exit. Is anyone even going to see you?

My husband and I thought that it wouldn't be romantic driving ourselves from the ceremony to the reception, but we just couldn't validate spending hundreds of dollars on something we were fully capable of doing ourselves. And it actually turned out to be the perfect choice. We were the last ones to leave the ceremony venue and arrive at the reception venue, so no one saw our "unromantic" exit or entrance, and it was nice being alone, quietly holding hands, without feeling like someone was watching us or listening to us talk.

If you really don't want to drive yourselves, ask a friend or family member to play chauffeur. It can be nice to have a quiet moment with someone (else) you love in the middle of the hustle and bustle of your Big Day.

3

Frugal Wedding

Food & Drinks

Food & Drinks

National Average Cost: $8,580

FEEDING YOUR GUESTS CAN BE A HUGE EXPENSE, especially if you have it catered. Catering companies typically charge per guest, and the average couple will spend $66 per plate. Some caterers don't even include dishes, ffatware, and serving your guests in their base charge.

Potluck Wedding
Your Frugal Wedding Budget: $300

While they may not be as popular now, potluck weddings have historically been the norm. People just didn't have the resources to feed everyone, so the whole community contributed. Nowadays, potluck weddings are a great alternative to expensive catering, as long as it's handled properly:

- **Don't run out of the main dish** - Even at potluck weddings, the couple often provides the main dish to make sure there is enough for everyone. If you're not going to take on that expense, make sure you get a few different people to bring the same thing to constitute the main entree, so no one's left hungry.

- **Keep it optional** - Not everyone is going to want to bring a dish, and some just won't be able to - you can't expect people who are traveling to cook. You don't want anyone feeling stressed about this, so include "Yes/No" check boxes on your invitation for bringing a dish.

- **Say goodbye to the registry** - If you're having a potluck wedding, etiquette demands that you drop the registry. People are saving you thousands of dollars by bringing food, so just accept that as your gift and buy your own toaster.

- **Keep it organized** - The biggest issue with potluck weddings is keeping the meal balanced. One way to do that is assign types of dishes by guests' first initials: A-D bring appetizers, E-H bring salads, I-L brings bread or dinner rolls, etc. Remember that redundancy is a good thing - you want multiple people bringing the same dish to ensure that everyone gets a balanced meal. Either you or someone on Team Wedding will need to keep track of the menu, monitoring the invitations and determining whether someone needs to switch dish types to avoid a pasta salad glut. Someone (not you or your sweetheart!) will also need to coordinate the day of, letting people know where to put their meals, making sure sternos are lit, confirming plates and flatware are abundant, and everything else that will make the meal run smoothly.

- **It's not free** - Even a potluck won't be completely free. Unless you're having your reception at a church or somewhere that already has supplies, you'll need to invest in serving utensils, plates, flatware, napkins, buffet pans, and sterno cans. And remember that even if you do have access to the venue's dishes, you could very well spend your first day of marriage of washing dishes, which may not cost anything, but isn't particularly romantic.

Keep Your Cash Tips

Afternoon Tea - Instead of a full meal, do an "afternoon tea" reception, offering snacks, hors d'oeuvres, and other flnger foods. You can prepare these simple foods the day before and refrigerate. It will be easy to accommodate the tastes of all your guests regardless of religious preferences or allergies. Children especially love these kinds of meals. You can also do a dessert-only reception, with a vast array of yummy sweets. This idea is great for rehearsal dinner as well (although you may not get away with doing it for both...)!

Build Your Own Meal Bars - Let your guests make their own meal with a taco bar, wafj e bar, or even a baked potato bar. This is a great way to display the food, and your guests will be happy because they can have their meal just the way they like it. Another benefit is that you don't need anyone to serve, because the guests serve themselves.

Food Truck - If you live near a city, chances are there are lots of amazing food trucks in your vicinity, and most would be thrilled to be hired for a private event. A food truck is perfect for catering outdoor receptions, and offer a wide variety of cuisine from tacos to crepes. They're also much cheaper than an actual caterer, and can offer a level of customization for your guests, although you'll want to limit the menu to just one or two options to keep your costs down. Check out food truck locator websites like RoamingHunger, or just take a walk around your city and sample different trucks. Obviously compare food quality, but also take note of kitchen cleanliness and servers' attitudes.

Backyard Barbecue - A grill and some coolers make a great party, no matter what the occasion. Grab a guy or gal who loves to grill and put them in charge of the hot dogs, hamburgers, or brats. Or go a bit more upscale and do a lobster boil or clambake on the beach. Ask your guests to bring sides such as fresh corn on the cob, homemade cole slaw, or fruit. Barbecues are perfect for the couple with laid back style, and they pair nicely with outdoor weddings.

DIY - Yes, you can even choose to feed your guests yourself! You'll spend money on the ingredients, but not nearly as much as if you used a caterer. Choose foods that can be made ahead and frozen to save yourself stress the day before the wedding. Good options include lasagna, soups, meatballs, spaghetti sauce, and meatloaf. Simply defrost and you're good to go. Stock up on ingredients ahead of time to spread the cost out over several months and take advantage of any sales. Make sure you have someone in charge of laying out the food so you don't have to worry about it on the Big Day.

Restaurant - Having your reception at a restaurant means you don't have to pay for servers, flatware, tables, or chairs. Find one that either has a nice decor already, or one that will allow you to bring in your own centerpieces, to ensure you get the ambience you're looking for.

Drinks/Alcohol - Alcohol is just plain expensive, and some venues charge you an extra fee if you plan to serve it at your wedding. You can save quite a bit of money skipping it entirely and let people toast with whatever they're drinking. If it's important to you, have a cash bar and let your guests know ahead of time. You could also provide a keg or a couple boxes of wine. Lots of couples are also opting to have a single "signature" drink, instead of an array of different alcohol. Buy drinks in bulk at a warehouse store such as BJ's or Sam's Club. (Coolers full of sodas and bottled water means that you don't need to buy cups.)

Plates and Flatware - A warehouse store comes in handy once again when it comes to setting the table. Many bulk stores have a selection of plates and flatware that are on the nicer side, and they will cost much less than what a caterer would charge. Plus, you get to keep any extras and use them at home!

Dessert

National Average Cost: $540+

When you think of a wedding cake, you probably imagine a frosted monstrosity of at least three tiers. The average wedding cake costs $540, and some couples even buy extra cakes to make sure there is enough for all of the guests. If you're doing a wedding on a budget, this just isn't an option.

Let Them Eat Sheet Cake...
Your Frugal Wedding Budget: $130

Cake is cake, am I right? Just buy a couple of sheet cakes from the grocery store - they might even pre-slice them for you if you ask nicely. Economical couples have been pulling the sheet cake switcheroo (getting a fancy cake for cutting, and then serving their guests sheet cake) for years anyway. Why not just pull back the curtain and reveal the truth: that you're too smart to spend $500 on a cake!

Keep Your Cash Tips

Shop Local - Check out small, locally owned bakeries to see if you can get a better deal. You might also flnd someone on CraigsList who bakes out of their home and will charge you far less than a larger cake shop. When ordering your cake, go for buttercream or cream cheese frosting instead of fondant; it's less expensive and tastes better!

Call a Friend - Have a friend or family member that enjoys time in the kitchen? Try to score a cake for free or for the cost of supplies and ingredients. It doesn't have to be a huge, elaborate cake to be memorable, and cake decorating has become a popular hobby.

Potluck It - If you're having a potluck dinner, why not the dessert too! You can either have a bunch of people bring the same thing, or just treat it like the rest of the potluck and let people choose their own dish.

Other Sweet Ideas - While cakes are traditional, other desserts are now trendy wedding alternatives. You could have wedding doughnuts, cookies, cheesecakes, or cupcakes. Five trays of pastries at your local bakery costs about the same as two sheet cakes, gives people more options, and eliminates the need for extra forks and plates.

4

Invitations

Invitations

National Average Cost: $440+

Invitations are the first impressions your guests will get of your wedding. Your guests will not only learn the date and time of your wedding, but how they should dress and whether or not they should come hungry. In short, they're a lot more than just a piece of paper.

Make Them Yourself
Your Frugal Wedding Budget: $75

Many word processing programs come with built-in templates for invitations that you can easily customize. Do a couple of test prints to make sure they look good before you print all of them. Pick up a few packages of blank cards that come with their own envelopes. If your printer can't handle the thicker paper, print it at an offlce supply store. Don't forget to triple-proofread (you, your flancee, and a friend) your invitations before printing - you don't want to have to pay twice for your supplies because of a single lousy typo!

You can also make your invitations with rubber stamps and other card making supplies from your local craft store. Get your friends or your flancee to help you and make a fun evening of it. Buy a chisel-tip marker and practice your "calligraphy" skills before addressing all of those envelopes, or just print out labels using a pretty font on your computer.

Either way you do it, keep your invitations easy to read, and ensure that they contain all of the information your guests will need. Stick with standard envelope sizes and keep the embellishments (ribbon, gems) to a minimum to avoid extra postage fees. Postage for postcards is even cheaper than sending invitations in envelopes, and are a particularly good idea if guests can RSVP electronically.

Keep Your Cash Tips

Skip Save the Dates - As soon as you have a hard date, contact the people you think may need an extra heads up by phone or email. As long as you get your invitations out to everyone else at least two or three months before your wedding, they should have enough time to make the necessary arrangements.

Go Electronic - In this day and age, there are lots of ways to reach your guests without using paper or postage. You can simply send out emails, but you need to make sure you send follow up reminders. There are also lots of websites that enable you to create a website specifically for your wedding, such as TheKnot, all for free. You can manage RSVPs, the menu, your registry, and any wedding-related information all in one central location. If emails seem too informal, make a fun video to send to everyone with the relevant details.

Remember that you probably have some guests, such as older relatives, who aren't comfortable responding electronically. You'll still need to get all of the information to them somehow, either with a phone call or a paper invitation.

RSVP - Even if you do send paper invitations, you can still cut down on your paper and postage costs by asking your guests to RSVP electronically. Set up a new email account or simply ask them to text or call. There are several RSVP websites available, but be careful to flnd one that's actually free.

5

Frugal Wedding

The Happy Couple

WHAT THE *HAPPY COUPLE* WEARS ON THE BIG DAY can take up a huge chunk of your overall budget. Most couples spend as much as 15% of their budget on the dress, tux, and rings.

It's also probably the most important of your expenses, because - there's no getting around it - everyone is going to be staring at you all day. Add onto that decades of looking at those pictures, and you definitely want to look your best. However, you're also going to be wearing these clothes for several hours (unless you change after the ceremony), so you need to be comfortable.

Let's break this down and see where we can start saving...

The Dress

National Average Cost: $1,200

It's easy to say that you're not going to spend more than "X" amount of dollars on your dress. But take a lesson from me: I made the mistake of settling for a less expensive dress that didn't fit quite right. Despite several sessions with the tailor (which, thank goodness, were included with the dress purchase - always ask about that!), I still didn't feel all that comfortable in the dress on the day of my wedding. So don't be afraid to spend a little more than you anticipated if it's going to make the difference between gazing fondly at your pictures after the fact, or spending your time cropping out unflattering armpit fat you didn't realize you had. Just make sure to accommodate for this change elsewhere in your overall budget.

Buy Used or Rent
Your Frugal Wedding Budget: $150

Buy Used - When buying a used dress, have a friend take your measurements so you know exactly what you need, as wedding dress sizes are often not the same as your regular clothing size. Also ask the seller about any alterations that have already been done, so you know exactly what you're getting.

The Bad News...

You are most likely not going to flnd your dream dress at a thrift store or yard sale, or on eBay or Craigslist. What you will flnd are tons and tons of inexpensive dresses that are beautiful but not your size, or have too many rufj es, or not enough lace.

The Good News...

Dresses can be tailored! Buying a $50 dress that is flve sizes too big and having it sized down can still be less expensive than a new dress. However, be sure to call around to local tailors with your list of expected alterations BEFORE you buy the dress to get an idea of how much it will cost. Sizing it down may only be $50, but adding or removing materials can cost a few hundred dollars, which defeats the purpose of buying a used dress.

And of course, don't forget that taking a dress in is usually an easy task, but letting one out may be impossible, so steer clear of dresses that are too small for you, even if you're on a wedding diet!

Rent - Why buy a dress at all? Websites such as Borrowing Magnolia, Nearly Newlywed, and Rent the Runway have all had good press about the high quality of their rentable dresses. Call up their customer service to flnd out exactly how it works to make sure you don't get zinged with any penalty fees for keeping a dress too long.

Keep Your Cash Tips

Borrow - You may not have to spend a dime if someone has a dress they're willing to loan or give you. After asking your mom, check around and see if an older cousin or aunt has a dress you can use. You're more likely to have luck with older relatives who are further away from their wedding day, as people closer to your age are probably still emotionally attached to and possessive of their gowns. Just make sure you double-check with your dress angel if you need to make alterations!

Clearance/Sample Sales - Bridal store sales are both good and bad. Obviously they're good because you're theoretically getting a better price on an expensive dress. They're bad because you really don't have the time to sit around and wait for a sale to buy your dress. Also, the selection will be limited, and items on clearance most likely do not come with any alterations, so you could still end up spending serious money on a tailor. You may also need to pay for dress cleaning out of pocket, which can be very expensive due to the fine fabrics and multiple layers.

Most wedding dress sales happen in late winter or early spring, when these retailers have to make room for the new dresses they've ordered for the coming season. If you're already past this point in the year, don't count on a sale as your saving grace. Go ahead and sign up for the email newsletters of all of the bridal boutiques in your area just in case, but don't stop looking elsewhere.

Etsy - While most likely more expensive than buying a used dress, a handmade dress by someone on Etsy will still be less expensive than bridal stores, especially if you have a simple design. A friend of mine had a kimono-style dress made on Etsy for $400, which isn't cheap, but she didn't need any alterations. Just be sure to triple-check your measurements, because most sellers won't do refunds for custom-made dresses.

Go Non-Traditional - When I was shopping for dresses, I had what I thought was the brilliant idea of going to department stores and just finding a nice white formal dress that wasn't labeled a "wedding dress." Well, I had no luck. I looked online. Still no luck.

I'm betting there's a secret understanding between these stores and the wedding industry to never have white formal wear, to avoid people such as myself circumventing the inflated cost of anything associated with weddings.

Arrgh!! Why is everything for weddings SO EXPENSIVE?!?!?!?

Anyway... My idea of a "non-traditional" wedding dress was actually pretty traditional, because I was still looking for white formal wear. Consider other colors, other styles. My sister got married in a white tank top and white skirt, and changed into shorts afterward to play volleyball with her guests, and still looked gorgeous.

Just remember that if you opt for a color other than white, you're not going to stand out as much, because no one wears white to a wedding, but they could wear green, pink, or red. To avoid blending in with the crowd too much, consider asking everyone else to wear white (or black and white) so you're the only one wearing color.

The Tux

National Average Cost: $250

Pretty much all of the strategies above apply to the tuxedo as well. Luckily, renting a tux is the standard for the groom, so it's not as much of a hassle as it is for the bride. However, consider going the non-traditional route to save even more.

Suit Up... or Not
Your Frugal Wedding Budget: $0

Does the groom already have a nice suit that flts well? If not, consider buying one. It may cost the same as a rental, but a suit is one of those things that comes in handy for future formal events, thus reducing your future expenses. He can always spice up his existing suit with a new vest, fancy cufj inks, or a French cuffi shirt.

If you're having a laid back or casual style wedding, let the groom join in the fun by wearing a nice button-down shirt and dress pants, which he should also already own.

The Rings

National Average Cost: $7,100+

Ah, the rings: symbols of your commitment to each other, of your eternal bond.

But that's all they are: a symbol. Any *specialness* attached to your wedding rings exists only because *you make them special.* Therefore, any ring from anywhere will do the trick, as long as it's of good quality and will last as long as your marriage.

Buy Used
Your Frugal Wedding Budget: $50

Engagement rings and wedding bands at retail jewelry stores can cost thousands of dollars. This is a perfect time to look for used bling on Tradesy, eBay, CraigsList, or even at local pawn shops. Even most online wedding ring retailers will have pre-owned sections with rings going for half the cost.

Unfortunately, rings at antique stores are usually pricey because they've gone from being "used" to that nebulous, somehow more valuable, label of "antique." And don't worry about that silly superstition that rings from an unsuccessful marriage are bad luck. It's not uncommon for women to sell their rings simply because they got new ones. Besides, you and your lovey are soulmates.

Remember, just because you're on a budget now, doesn't mean you'll always be on one. Someday you and your sweetheart will be feeling more prosperous, and you can "surprise" each other with a new set as an anniversary gift (after you've both had fun shopping for your favorites...).

If you're really hoping for fancy-looking new rings, you can flnd knockoffidesigner wedding rings on eBay, and unique or non-traditional rings on Etsy or Amazon. If you do buy a ring online, make sure you triple-check your ring size at a local jeweler. Some rings can be sized within reason, but it doesn't always turn out well depending on how the ring was made. Also check if there are any reviews for the ring, and learn from others who have been burned by cheap workmanship.

Shoes & Other Accessories

National Average Cost: $250+

Don't forget to budget for shoes, jewelry, veils, crowns, or whatever else the bride wants as part of her attire. "Bridal" shoes can retail for $200+, which is pretty ridiculous. Remember our guiding principle of thinking about what you can use after the wedding, and try to flnd fancy shoes that you will wear with other outflts.

Or...

Raid Your Closet
Your Frugal Wedding Budget: $0

Keep it simple, using accessories you already own or can borrow (something borrowed: check!), and your bank account will thank you.

6

Frugal Wedding

Hair and Makeup

Hair and Makeup

National Average Cost: $200+

THERE'S NO DOUBT YOU WANT TO FEEL MAGICAL on your wedding day, and your hair and makeup are just as much a part of that as your dress. If you decide to have a professional help you, it's likely to cost over $200 between both a trial run appointment and the actual wedding day appointment. Whether or not this expense is worth it depends on what you envision yourself looking like on the Big Day, and whether you have a stylist you can trust to do what you want. If you're terrible at hair and makeup, then it might be a good thing to budget for.

Do It Yourself
Your Frugal Wedding Budget: $0

You know how you like your makeup to look. While many brides think they need something completely different to be glamorous, this isn't necessarily true. A little extra eye makeup and a new shade of lipstick can be just enough to edge you into princess status. You want to wear enough makeup to look good for pictures, but not so much that it's embarrassing for your guests to see you in real life.

The same goes for your hair. You've been styling your hair for most of your life, so you're familiar with its texture and natural part. You also know what it will and won't do. This gives you more of an advantage than you realize. Try different styles and wear them around for the day to see how they hold up. A hair style that falls down after an hour is only going to cause you frustration. Make sure you pick a look that fits well with your current cut and the texture of your hair for best results.

For both your hair and your makeup, check out the numerous tutorials available on YouTube. Make sure you practice your style choice several times well before the Big Day.

Ask a Friend - Once again, your friends and family can come to the rescue here! Do you have an aunt that runs a beauty salon? Or a friend that had gone to school for cosmetology before she decided to be a nurse instead? Pull on the talents of those around you, and you can probably flnd someone who can do it for free. You still need to make sure that you have a couple of practice sessions to ensure you achieve your desired look and that it will hold up.

7

Frugal Wedding

Bridesmaids & Groomsmen

ALTHOUGH NOT TECHNICALLY PART OF YOUR wedding budget, since the wedding party usually pays for their own dresses and tuxes, you can still help them save money too. After all, you're probably not the only one on a budget. Plus, if you keep them from having to pay hundreds of dollars on clothes, you may get an even better wedding present...

Let your bridesmaids' personalities shine too - With low-budget and highly personalized weddings as the norm these days, identical dresses for the bridesmaids is less expected. Pull from your wedding color scheme and just ask all the bridesmaids to stick to the same color and style (e.g. calf-length lavender dress). This allows your bridesmaids to select dresses that work with their body types, instead of forcing a one-size-flts-all ideal.

Note that this strategy will only work as long as your colors are simple. Black and white? They've got it covered. Dark magenta and cyan? Maybe not so much. If you have a very speciflc and off-shade color scheme, consider giving them swatches to shop with.

Department Stores - Bridal stores aren't the only places with pretty dresses. Browse through the formal section of your local department store. This is an especially good resource for junior bridesmaids and fflower girls when holiday dresses go on clearance. Even the full price is likely to be less than half of what you would flnd at a bridal retailer.

Go Casual - Be open to outflts that aren't as formal. This can provide a fun atmosphere to your wedding, and they will deflnitely be less expensive than formalwear. Bridesmaids can wear skirts or sundresses, and groomsmen can wear suits, button-down shirts, or even t-shirts. As long as it flts with your colors and the vibe of your Big Day, go for it.

8

Frugal Wedding

Centerpieces, Favors, & Decor

Decor

National Average Cost: $2,000

MOST VENUES WILL NEED A LITTLE SPRUCING UP. Centerpieces and other decorations not only look nice, but also bring the whole room together with your wedding theme. But when you add up the cost of centerpieces from a florist, decorations for the food tables, and any other trimmings such as pew bows, it can get pretty pricey.

Do It Yourself
Your Frugal Wedding Budget: $50

This is one place where your (or a friend's) DIY skills will really come in handy. This is the perfect time to have your friends and family over for a centerpiece-making party. Choose centerpieces that don't require fresh fflowers so you can make them ahead of time. Making centerpieces that can double as guest favors is a great money-saving strategy as well.

Not sure what to do? Here are just a few ideas that use low- or no-cost materials:

- mason jars or vases with ffoating tea lights or candles in sand
- inffated balloons wrapped in tulle and tied down with ribbon
- potted plants (grow them yourself and they're even cheaper!)
- cut up thick tree branches into discs and put a single, large fflower head in the middle
- bowls of fruit
- gourds
- paper lanterns
- stacks of books
- framed artistic photographs of places or things you both love
- succulents

- create your own wedding "logo" (monogram or graphic icon) and stencil, stamp, and print it onto everything wedding-related; this can make items that may not look the same still feel cohesive

Keep Your Cash Tips

Ceremony Decorations - An arch is nice, but not necessary. If you do decide that this is a must-have, check Craigslist or Facebook swap groups to see if you can flnd one used. Or take a peek at Pinterest for other backdrop ideas.

Hit the Lights - Christmas lights are a great addition to food tables, arches, and other decorations. You probably have plenty hiding in your basement. The ones with white wires (as opposed to green) typically work the best for tables and arches, but the green ones are flne if you're weaving them into greenery or decorative trees.

Outdoor Wedding = Less Decorations - Having your wedding in a setting that is already full of fflowers and naturally beautiful scenery, like a park, garden nursery, or botanical center, will significlantly reduce your decorating budget. Even if the venue is a bit more expensive, compare it to the cost of decorations and see which is actually cheaper.

Favors

National Average Cost: $280+

While you could try to get away without giving favors, this is one of the best ways to let your personality as a couple shine, and there are plenty of ways to do so creatively and inexpensively.

Escort Card Favors
Your Frugal Wedding Budget: $50

A great way to save money is for your escort cards to double as favors. You can also give one favor per couple for added savings. Here are a few ideas:

- **Mix CDs** - Fill these with your (and your sweetie's) favorite tunes. Use paper CD envelopes and find someone with nice handwriting and a chiseled marker to write the names and seating arrangements on the back.

- **Wine Glasses** - Frequent thrift stores for wine glasses on the cheap, and tie the place cards to stems with ribbon. This will only really work if you have wine at your wedding though... And don't forget to wash them!
- **Candy Buffet** - Make a table of candies in your wedding colors, and give each guest a personalized baggie. Let them create their own perfect and sweet favor.
- **Keep it Useful** - Whatever you decide to use for favors, it will still be a waste of your money and/or time if people don't take them home. Edible or practical gifts are the best route, rather than fancy and frivolous.
- **Centerpieces** - I know I said it already, but just in case you missed it: centerpieces can double as favors as well!

Guest Book

National Average Cost: $60

While the guest book is not the most notable expense on any wedding list, it's deflnitely an expense worth scrutinizing. Any pretty blank book you like will do - just make sure it will lay ffat easily.

Or how about you...

Get Creative
Your Frugal Wedding Budget: $20

There are lots of new, non-traditional, and low-cost ideas for guest "books":

- puzzle pieces
- poster
- large photo matte that you can use later for your wedding photo
- flnd a used photography book fllled with pictures that go with the theme of your wedding - people can sign the inside covers, or on the pages themselves
- buy the album you're going to use for your wedding pictures or scrapbook before the Big Day, and have your guests get it started for you by signing all over
- baseball caps
- Jenga pieces
- a pretty piece of fabric or quilt

Card Box or Wishing Well
Your Frugal Wedding Budget: $5

A cardboard box covered in pretty paper costs next to nothing!

If you do decide to purchase a box or bird cage, make sure it's one that you'd like to see on your mantle when the wedding is over.

9

Frugal Wedding

Flowers

Flowers

National Average Cost: $2,000+

FLOWERS CAN HELP GIVE YOUR VENUE A MORE romantic atmosphere. They'll also be featured in almost all of your photographs, so it's important to flnd ones that flt your style and taste. In addition to a bridal bouquet, you may also want bridesmaids' bouquets; boutonnieres for the groom, groomsmen, ring bearer, and fathers; corsages for the mothers; and petals for the ffower girl. Don't forget the toss bouquet! It really adds up, but the great thing is that there are lots of ways to get beautiful ffowers on a budget.

Grow and Arrange Them Yourself
Your Frugal Wedding Budget: $20

A true do-it-yourself idea is to check out what flowers are in bloom around your wedding date and grow them yourself! All you have to buy are the seeds or bulbs. This works even better if you or a family member already has a garden with well-established flowering plants, such as hydrangeas, lilacs, or tulips.

A close alternative to growing them is buying them at the Farmer's Market, depending on what time of year you're getting married. They are usually far cheaper than you would find at any stores, and they're from local farms.

If arranging fresh flowers yourself, make sure you leave yourself plenty of time the night before your wedding to do it. If you think you'll be too busy the night before, ask a friend.

Keep Your Cash Tips

Less is More - Instead of giving each of your bridesmaids an entire bouquet, give them just one flower - just make sure it's big and bright enough to stand out.

Double Duty - If you do get bouquets for you and the bridesmaids, consider using them again as centerpieces. Assign someone the task of collecting all of them after the ceremony and dropping them into the empty vases before everyone else shows up at the reception.

Skip the Florist - Grocery stores have the same fflowers as fflorist boutiques for a fraction of the price. Some might even make the bouquets for you.

Use Artificial Flowers - Silk or other fabric fflowers are a great alternative for those who want to keep things easy and inexpensive. You can arrange them months in advance, with plenty of time to decide what looks good. You'll never have to worry about keeping them fresh, and the wedding party can keep their bouquets and boutonnieres as keepsakes. Watch the sales fflyers at your local craft stores to get artif
lcial fflowers for a discounted price.

Don't Use Them - While many people expect fflowers at a wedding, it doesn't mean you have to use them. You can make lots of great centerpieces that don't include fflowers, using vases, candles, stones, signs, etc. Even bridal bouquets can be made out of other items, including feathers and vintage brooches.

You can also make your own "flowers" out of pretty paper or even coffee filters, if you'd like.

10

Frugal Wedding

Officiant

Officiant

National Average Cost: $260+

THIS IS ONE PART OF YOUR WEDDING THAT YOU can't do yourself! Depending on where you live and your religious preferences, it can be hard to find someone to officiate your wedding. The best way to start is with a simple online search for officiants in your area. This will pull up several wedding vendor sites where you can check out their credentials and reviews and see if they're willing to travel to your venue. This is also a great source if you're looking for alternative officiants that will provide non-religious ceremonies.

No matter where you find an officiant, spend some time talking to them and making sure they can provide the service you're looking for. Ministers or other religious officials may be a little be more conservative or have certain rules they must follow that don't fit in with your dream wedding, so ask for specific details. If you can, get a copy of the ceremony in writing. This ensures that everyone is on the same page, and it gives you and your fiancee a chance to go over it in detail.

Ask A Friend
Your Frugal Wedding Budget: $0

The American Fellowship Church, Universal Life Church, along with other online ministries, will ordain just about anyone to officiate a wedding. HOWEVER, call the registrar in the township where your wedding will be held before your friend becomes ordained, because municipalities can vary as to whom they legally recognize as a wedding officiant.

Keep Your Cash Tips

Courthouse or Town/City Hall - Give your local courthouse or city hall a call. They may be able to direct you to a low cost justice of the peace, notary public, officiant, or retired judge who can perform the ceremony.

Explore Within Your Faith - If you and/or your fiancee are religious, you can probably find someone within your church who is willing to help you out, either for free or a small fee.

11

Frugal Wedding

The Photographer

Photographer

National Average Cost: $2,400+

IF YOU'VE PRICED OUT WEDDING PHOTOGRAPHERS, you already know that this aspect of your wedding can blow your modest budget in an instant. But this is one of the few wedding aspects that definitely can't be done by you, and really can't be done by a family member or friend either because you want them in the pictures too! So how do you have a $1500 wedding without spending it all on a photographer?

Find a Beginner
Your Frugal Wedding Budget: $200

Consider finding a photographer on CraigsList or at a local college who is just starting out. Often he or she will be happy to do your wedding for a couple hundred dollars just to build their portfolio. Ideally, they will already have at least a few samples of their work for you to look at, which will make you feel more comfortable with hiring them.

Keep Your Cash Tips

Friends of Friends - Photography is a very popular hobby these days. Ask everyone you know to ask everyone they know to try to find someone who is an amateur photographer who would be willing to shoot your wedding for a couple hundred dollars. Be sure to ask:

- to see samples of their portrait work, either on social media or via email
- what kind of camera they use, to make sure it's a high-end digital
- when and how they will send you your pictures

Keep It Short - Reduce the amount of billable hours for your photographer by scheduling important events like toasts, cutting the cake, and tossing the bouquet as early in the reception as possible. That way the photographer can get all of the shots you need and leave, rather than staying for the entire evening.

Fight for Your Right... to Print? Many wedding photographers will charge you for their services, and then make you pay again for the right to get prints. Of your photos. Of YOUR wedding.

The thing is, technically they have the right to do that, because photography is covered by intellectual property laws: Whoever takes the picture owns all of the rights to that picture.

What that means, is that when hiring a wedding photographer - especially if they're an amateur or beginner - you have to make it clear that you want a USB or DVD with all of the digital images taken on your Big Day, along with an understanding (perhaps even in writing) that you have the right to print any and all of those pictures as many times as your big wonderful heart desires. Remember that the photographer will still retain intellectual ownership of those pictures, however, and - especially if they are a beginner - they will likely use pictures from your wedding on their website.

Edit, Print, and Scrapbook Yourself - Even beginner photographers will most likely charge you extra for editing your photos. Prints and albums will also cost you extra if ordered through your photographer - far more than getting them printed at WalMart, CVS, or online printing websites like SnapFish and Picaboo. Let whoever is taking your pictures know that you will handle all of this yourself, and all you want from them are HIGH-RESOLUTION digital files.

A Group Effort - In today's current age of smartphones, you can also provide a few close friends or family with a specific list of simple pictures you'd like taken (cake, guests seated, sweetheart table, centerpieces, etc.). Be careful though - this should be a COMPLEMENT to your hired photographer, NOT a replacement. This day is just too important to miss capturing it on film. A friend of mine opted for the "disposable cameras on the tables" route, and she ended up with about a hundred pictures of her and her new husband walking into their reception and not much else.

Know What You Want - Whoever does your photography, do some research and make note of shots and poses that you like, and share them with your photographer. Even the experts like a little insight into exactly what you want. The only way to get that perfect shot is to let everyone know about it beforehand.

Make a Schedule - Keep in mind that there are probably a lot of pictures that you would like to have taken, and it might be difficult to squeeze it all in during your wedding. You'll miss out on time mingling with your guests and enjoying the party. Consider having the wedding portraits taken before the ceremony when the other guests haven't arrived yet. Note that this doesn't work if you are a traditional couple and you don't want to see each other before the ceremony.

Another key problem when it comes to wedding portraits is making sure everyone is there when you need them. Let both sides of the family know when they'll be needed for pictures. You don't have time to be chasing down soon-to-be in-laws!

12

Frugal Wedding

The Music

Music

National Average Cost: $5,000+

EVER SINCE YOU WERE LITTLE, YOU'VE DREAMED of your first dance as a married couple - but you probably never worried about who would be in charge of playing the music. Music provides a soundtrack for your wedding, with songs that are important to you and say something about your relationship. Paying for a wedding band or a DJ can take a hefty chunk out of any budget, but we live in a time where you have other options.

Digital DJ

Your Frugal Wedding Budget: $0

Many brides-to-be are skipping the formality of an actual DJ and simply downloading their favorite music onto an iPod or other digital device. Then you just have to bring in a speaker or two and hit play! If you do decide to have an iPod wedding, make sure you have someone assigned to manage it. Just because you have all the perfect songs loaded onto it doesn't mean they'll play exactly when you need them to. Ask a friend or family member who's familiar with the device to be in charge of the soundtrack for your wedding. Also, make sure the songs are loaded onto a playlist in the correct order so there's less chance of a mess-up.

Keep Your Cash Tips

DJ on the Cheap - Check Craigslist or other local listings for college students who might be willing to DJ for a few bucks and a free meal. You can also try calling university campus centers and asking if they've hired any student DJs recently.

Live Music - Wedding bands can be a lot of fun but are very expensive. Luckily, there are a lot of options that are easier on your budget:

- *Less is More* - Instead of going straight for a group of musicians, consider one or two instruments. Why hire a full string quartet for your ceremony when you can get just as much romance and fullness of sound with a solo cello? You may need to pay a little extra because the musician has to do all of the work, but it will still be less than an ensemble. Just pick your instrument wisely: A harp may look and sound ethereal and romantic, but it's actually generally more expensive because of the hassle of transportation.

- *Local Talent* - Decide what kind of music you want (jazz, rock, traditional folk music, classical, etc.) and then call around to local bars, restaurants, and clubs to find out if there are any groups performing in your genre of choice. If you like what you hear, approach them about performing at your wedding. Be sure to ask where they're based - musicians will often charge more if they have to travel more than an hour to get to your venue.

- *Local Schools* - Call up music schools in your area and ask if there are any faculty who are interested, or any students who have the professionalism and performance capability. Be sure to meet with any students before giving them the gig, and don't be afraid to ask them to play for you as an audition.

13

Frugal Wedding

Rehearsal Dinner & Post-Wedding Brunch

Rehearsal Dinner & Post-Wedding Brunch

National Average Cost: $1,100+

AS MUCH AS WE'D LIKE TO SKIP THE EXPENSE, rehearsal the day before is necessary. If you want your day to run smoothly and stress-free, then you definitely need to get everyone in the wedding party together to run through the logistics. This is particularly important if friends and family will be helping with things like table and chair setup, music duties, and officiating. At the same time, the post-wedding brunch is a perfect way to thank out-of-town guests for traveling, and say goodbye. Unfortunately, both of these activities can cost a lot, and these costs need to be included in your wedding budget.

The good news is that lots of the same cost-saving strategies that apply to your wedding can also help you save on your rehearsal dinner and brunch.

BYOBBQ
Your Frugal Wedding Budget: $100

A backyard Bring Your Own Barbecue works for either the rehearsal or as a replacement for the brunch. You buy the burgers, and ask everyone else to bring everything else. It's a great way for everyone to relax just before (or after) the Big Day, and it is loads cheaper than a traditional formal meal.

Keep Your Cash Tips

Bare Essentials Guest List - The rehearsal dinner has ballooned in recent years into an event including nearly as many people as the wedding day itself. For those Happy Couples keeping their costs low, the only people you should invite to your rehearsal dinner are those in the wedding party.

Depending on the number of out-of-town guests you

have, you might be able to include them too; if there are too many to invite, let them know that you're keeping the rehearsal dinner to wedding party and immediate families only, and you'll be having a post-wedding brunch that they're invited to. You can even limit the brunch to out-of-towners only, or out-of-towners and immediate family only, leaving out bridesmaids and groomsmen, since you probably see them all the time anyway.

Skip the Full Meal - Schedule your rehearsal earlier in the day. Get a bunch of friends together the day before and make flnger sandwiches and brownies. Afternoon tea is a perfect theme for this type of gathering.

Leftovers - If you took home a refrigerator's worth of leftovers from your wedding, invite everyone over to help you clear it all out, rather than spending money on a post-wedding brunch.

Think Outside the Dinner Box - Instead of feeding everyone, pay for a fun night or afternoon at the bowling alley or mini golf range. Or go the free route: pack up the bocce ball or cornhole set and have everyone join you for a BYOP (picnic) at a nearby park. Activities like this are a relaxing and unique way for the in-laws and wedding party to get to know each other better. If it's your rehearsal, you might have trouble getting everyone to focus on the task at hand, so you might want to get the logistics out of the way *before* blowing them all away with your kickball skills.

14

Frugal Wedding

Final Thoughts

Greenback Wedding

IT'S NOT POSSIBLE TO TALK ABOUT YOUR WEDDING budget without talking about having a "greenback" wedding; meaning, asking for cash from your guests instead of traditional gifts. Some tactful ways of asking for money include:

- *Word of Mouth* - Tell friends and family that if anyone asks them, you'd like cash instead of gifts.
- *Online Cash Registries* - There are lots of websites that offer cash registries, like Honeyfund or MyRegistry, and these are a great way to direct your guests to specific

goals you'd appreciate some help funding (like your honeymoon!).

- *Keep it Optional* - Some guests will still want to get you a regular gift, so create a traditional online gift registry as well. Be thoughtful with your gift registry; this is a great way to suggest items that you would have spent money on anyway, freeing up more of your cash for you and your sweetie's new life together.

Let's Recap

Here's the same chart from Chapter One, outlining the excessive national average costs of a wedding:

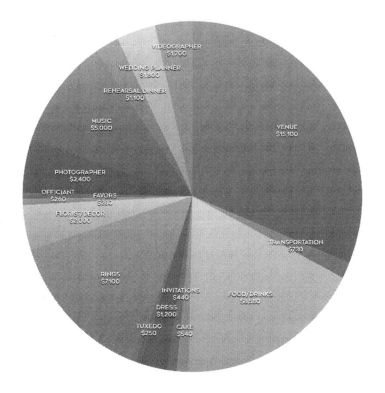

National Average Wedding Costs in the USA

Now, here's a chart outlining the costs of *Your Frugal Wedding* Budget:

venue - $300

tables/chairs - $50

transportation - $0

food/drinks - $300

cake - $130

invitations - $75

dress - 150

tux - $0

rings - $50

shoes/accessories - $0

decor - $50

favors - $50

guest book - $20

card box - $5

flowers - $20

officiant - $0

photographer - $200

music - $0

rehearsal dinner/post-wedding brunch - $100

=$1500

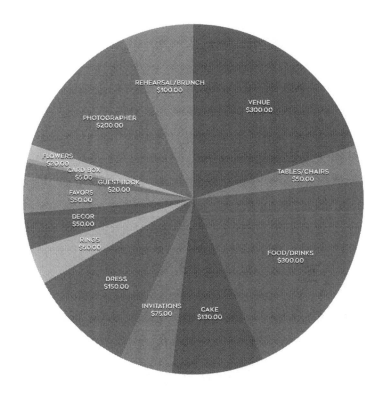

REHEARSAL/BRUNCH
$100.00

VENUE
$300.00

PHOTOGRAPHER
$200.00

FLOWERS
$20.00

CARD BOX
$5.00

GUEST BOOK
$20.00

TABLES/CHAIRS
$50.00

FAVORS
$50.00

DECOR
$50.00

RINGS
$50.00

FOOD/DRINKS
$300.00

DRESS
$150.00

INVITATIONS
$75.00

CAKE
$130.00

Your Frugal Wedding Costs

Much better!

Again, everything on here is fluid depending on your priorities, opportunities, and connections. Know someone who can shoot your wedding for free? Score! Add that $200 to your dress budget. Did your father-in-law offer to pay for the venue? Cool! Maybe you can hire that solo acoustic guitarist for the ceremony! The goal of this book is to show you that it truly is possible to have a fun, romantic wedding and not pay for it later. Literally.

Good Luck!

Does it seem like there's an awful lot to think about and way too many decisions to make? Relax. That's how every couple feels regardless of their budget. Just make sure you set aside a little bit of time each week to discuss arrangements or do some shopping, and you'll have it all put together in no time.

This book has shown you many ways to save money for your wedding. There is no part of a wedding that you can't get for a better price, or perhaps even for free. Don't settle on anything that costs more than you're willing to pay. After all, it's your money and your day!

The bottom line here is that you should not feel ashamed or stressed because you want your wedding to come in at a reasonable amount. Budget weddings are far more common than you may realize, and they are a product of careful planning and great amounts of personal effort. It may take a little more time, but it's definitely worth it.

Having an economical wedding does not mean that

you have to make sacrifices on aesthetics, fun, or style. If anything, it means that you have put a little bit more time and effort into each aspect of your wedding, choosing elements that reflect your personalities.

So invite your friends and family to help you, seek out the best available prices for everything, and start planning. Remember, every penny you save can be put towards your fun honeymoon getaway!

And congratulations again! Thank you, and good luck!

Frugal Wedding

Frugal Wedding Resources

Amazon Warehouse Deals

FatWallet

My Wedding Favors

Online Wedding Registry

Raise

and our own site:

YOUR FRUGAL WEDDING:

www.yourfrugalwedding.com

Frugal Wedding

About the Author

Rachel Hathaway is the pen name for a professional writer whom you may or may not know (Mysterious, huh?). Her work spans many areas of creative flction -- including the very wide romance genre -- as well as her published non-flction self-help guides, personal growth and development ebooks, and a large number of articles and posts across the web on a variety of sites and blogs about smart modern shopping, style, music, the arts, and a range of eco-friendly topics. She lives in New England with her devoted in their dream home, and they make sure to enjoy the wonderful aspects of life on a daily basis.

Finally, if you enjoyed this book, please take the time to share your thoughts and post a review where you

bought it, because most people don't. If you do, it'd be greatly appreciated!

For more information and to join our mailing list:

www.yourfrugalwedding.com

Also by Rachel Hathaway

Updated Paleo Diet Food List (Plus Paleo Diet Shopping Lists) [*Also in paperback, audiobook, and in Spanish and Danish ebook translations*]

Beginner's Guide to Writing and Self-Publishing Romance eBooks (New Romance Writer Series) [*Also in paperback*]

Minimalism for Moms: Simplify, Declutter, and Organize Your Way to a Stress Free and Meaningful Life (Serenity at Home)

The Unofficial History of Flirting: Plus Five Ways to Reinvent Valentine's Day and Flirt Like a Bird! (Sassy Girl Series) [*Also in paperback*]

SPANISH TRANSLATIONS (with Elisa Prada, translator):

Lista de alimentos para la dieta Paleo: Actualizado / Spanish Language Edition (Updated Paleo Diet Food List Book) (Serie de Nutrición) (Spanish Edition) [*Also in paperback*]

Minimalismo para Mamás: Simplifica, arregla, y organiza tu camino hacia una vida plena libre de estrés (Minimalism for Moms / Spanish edition) (Serie Serenidad en el Hogar)

Frugal Wedding

NOTES & IDEAS:

Made in the USA
Middletown, DE
19 June 2017